Say Cheese

Healthy Gourmet Recipes
with Dutch Cheese

To Eve,
Enjoy life to the fullest!
Yvonne Stephens

by Chef Yvonne Stephens, CC

Say Cheese

Published by US Design

3 Justa Lane

Cherry Hill, New Jersey 08003

For more information about our books, please write to us, or call 856-489-4313,

or visit our website at

www.getrealhealthyfood.com

Research & Recipes: Yvonne Stephens

Graphic Design & Foodstyling: Yvonne Stephens

Photography: John A. Stephens Jr.

ISBN-13: 978-0-9765762-0-4

Copyright© 2007 by Yvonne Stephens

About the author

Yvonne Stephens is a chef, former fitness instructor, and world-traveler. She holds a culinary science degree from the Art Institute of Philadelphia and works as an author, chef, and food stylist. Stephens spends all her free time visiting new places, trying new cuisines, and learning more about healthy, delicious eating.

Her passion for cooking comes from both her grandmother and mother, who prepared traditional Dutch meals every day. She learned that cooking your own food at home is the cornerstone of 'healthy nutrition.' In her first book, "Amazing 7 Minute Meals", Chef Yvonne has transformed a wide range of world cuisines into quick and easy to prepare stir-fry meals.

Holland is one of the primary dairy countries of Europe, and cheese is an important part of Dutch nutrition. As an original 'cheesehead', Yvonne eats cheese almost every day, but her philosophy is, eat a small piece of good cheese rather than a large piece, with little flavor.

"Health and healthy eating are very important to me, and that is what I hope to teach the people, who purchase my books. These cheese recipes were created for healthy and delicious eating." Good cheese brings great flavor to simple and easy-to-make dishes.

All the "Say Cheese" recipes were created using Dutch cheeses; like Gouda, Edam, Boerenkaas, Delft Blue and Beemster® brand cheeses. "The assortment of Beemster® Cheese is just the best," says Chef Yvonne. From young Gouda style cheese, to an older Classic, or the oldest XO, these cheeses really offer the best of traditional Dutch cheese making." Beemster® is the only Netherlands cheese company to receive the Appointment to the Royal Court of The Netherlands. Their specialty cheeses; like Lite, Garlic, Mustard, or Nettle are great for the both novice and connoisseur.

Thanks to Beemster® Cheese, for the usage of their cow and farm photos.

Recipe *Index*

Recipe *Index* continued

Just *Say Cheese!*

Cheese is nothing more than milk with a long shelf life. And, how was cheese invented? Well, a cow gives milk for their calves, and by prolonging the lactation period, the cow gives more milk, which can be used to make cheese. But, how did we find out that milk could be made into cheese?

The legend is that an unknown nomad carried milk in a stomach of a cow (plastic bags were not available yet) wrapped in an animal skin bag, which was tied to the saddle of his horse. The movement caused the fermentation of the milk sugars, so the milk curdled, breaking up the curd and separating the whey.

The nomad discovered that the whey was a refreshing drink and the curd a nourishing food, high in protein with a much longer shelf (saddle) life than any other protein.

Through the ages, the balanced methods and techniques improved, but basically, the whole procedure never changed.

Through time, various cheeses were created:

Cheese	Country	Year
Gorgonzola	Italy	879
Roquefort	France	1070
Grana	Italy	1200
Edam	Holland	1450
Gouda	Holland	1679

Cheese was the product of local farms, which often had no more than 1 or 2 cows, with just a small amount of milk per farm. Groups of Dutch farmers from all over the North of the country joined together in co-ops. By the end of the 19th century 'dagfabriekjes' (day manufacture) was a new, more efficient way to produce cheese.

These days, cheese making is totally modernized and uses machines, with the exception of a select group of cheese makers in the world. For this book, I went to visit a great example of a company, making cheese in the traditional way.

Cono Cheesemakers are the makers of Beemster® cheese, and as the cheese wheels are set aside for aging, each wheel is continually turned and polished with love and care.

This process ensures a perfect texture and wonderful flavor in every Beemster cheese. Similar cheese is available, but people complain that 'the good old-fashion taste is gone".

The reason for that is enhancement of the maturing process, which means enzymes are used to reduce the time for the cheese to mature. When these enzymes are used, the cheese has a kind of a 'tingling' after-taste.

Beemster farmers still take the pledge that their forefathers made very seriously. Absolutely no pesticides of any kind are used on the pastures today, and the farmers also believe that natural cows make the best milk. All cows are left to graze freely at least 10 months out of the year, and are never injected with any form of growth hormones.

Gouda is the name of a city in Holland, which became famous due to the name of the cheese. The most important basis of that popularity is the traditional quality control and fat content of 48%. Beemster is a type of Gouda cheese. Cheese named after other Dutch cities and areas are: Edam (40% fat), Leyden (cumin cheese), Maaslander (Dutch Swiss cheese) and Old Amsterdam (fast matured).

The flavor of cheese increases in strength while ripening:

Jong (young)	4 weeks
Jong Belegen (young, slightly mature)	8 weeks
Belegen (Mature)	4 months
Extra Belegen (Extra Mature)	7 months
Oud (Old-Aged)	from 10 months
Overjarig (More then 1 year)	from 12 months
Brokkel (Crumble)	from 24 months>

Cheese is made of more types of milk than just cow. Here is a synopsis of types of cheese:

Cow – Gouda, Brie, Camembert, Cheddar, etc.

Buffalo – Mozzarella. Buffalo milk is fat-free and contains a higher percentage of milk sugars.

Horse – These days, horse milk is rarely being used, except to make the yogurt-like cheese.

Goat – Chèvre, Gouda Goat Cheese, Chevagne, Buche Chêvre, Lingo Cendré, Crottin.

Sheep – Roquefort, Marival, Pecorino Toscano, Manchego Arte Queso, Brique de Pays, Brebi.

People with lactose intolerance can eat sheep and goat cheese and the older Gouda types like Beemster® Classic and XO.

Ham & *Cheese* Puff Pastry Fun

Makes 6

A great snack, breakfast item, or party hors d'oeuvres. Easy to prepare and only needs a short oven time. Be creative with shapes and filling.

Ingredients:
- 1 puff pastry sheet, 10x10 inch, rolled out to 12x12 inch, cut into squares or triangles
- 6 slices smoked ham
- 12 slices mature cheese, like Beemster® Classic cheese
- Eggwash: 1 egg, 1 teaspoon milk, beaten with basting brush

1 - Pre-heat oven to 375°F/190°C.

2 - Cut pastry sheets into desired shapes. Place 1 slice of ham and 2 slices of cheese on each shape, add top pastry. Press edges together, brush with eggwash.

3 - Place on cookie sheet or baking stone.

4 - Place in the oven for ± 20 minutes or until golden brown. Serve immediately.

TIP: This recipe is also delicious with Dutch blue cheese or a smooth goat cheese.

Sparkling Wine

The bubbles make you pick the stars at broad daylight. Impart your unforgettable moments with the fizz of champagne. Only the sparkling wine from the Champagne region in France is allowed to carry the name Champagne. It is called Cava in Spain, Prosecco in Italy and Sekt in Germany, and you can choose from Dry, Extra Dry, Brut, Blanc or Rosé.

9

Corn &  Cheese Delights

Serves 4

Satisfaction guaranteed with this delicious combination of Mother Nature's ingredients.

Ingredients Corn & Cheese Soup:

- ½ Tablespoon oil • 4 ears of corn, grilled, kernels cut off or 6 cups canned or frozen corn kernels • 1 quart chicken or vegetable stock
- 4 slices bacon, crisped in the oven, chopped, save a few small pieces
- ½ cup onion, chopped • 1 hot pepper, chopped
- 2 cups skim milk or Half & Half
- 1 cup grated spiced cheese, like Beemster® Garlic cheese
- Salt & pepper to taste
- Cilantro leaves for garnish

  1 - Place ½ Tablespoon oil in the skillet. Sauté the onion and hot pepper until lightly caramelized.

  2 - Add stock, corn, milk, bring to a boil, and let simmer for 5 minutes.

  3 - Using a slotted spoon, place ¾ of the mixture in a blender and puree. Return mixture to pan, add bacon and season with a little salt and pepper.

  4 - Serve with ¼ cup grated Garlic cheese on top of each bowl, and garnish with a few pieces of bacon and cilantro leaves.

Ingredients corn bread:

- 2 cups corn meal
- 3 Tablespoons wheat flour
- ½ teaspoon sugar
- ½ Tablespoon salt • pinch red crushed pepper
- 2 Tablespoons bell pepper, chopped
- 1 cup grated young cheese, like Beemster® Vlaskaas, save a small handful for topping.

  1 - Pre-heat oven to 375°F/190°C. Mix all ingredients.

  2 - Grease a bread tin or muffin tin with the bacon drippings, using a basting brush.

  3 - Place in the oven for ± 20 minutes or until golden brown.

Belgium *Endive* Gratin

Serves 2

A real comfort food which is on many countries' favorites list.

Ingredients:

- 4 Belgium endives • 4 slices of ham
- 1 cup grated old cheese, like Beemster® XO cheese
- 2 Tablespoons white wine • Salt & pepper to taste

  1 - Remove bottom of Belgium endives. Boil them for 5 minutes, drain.

  2 - Roll them in a slice of ham. Place in an oven-safe dish. Add white wine and a pinch of salt and pepper.

  3 - Divide grated cheese over the Belgium endives and place in a pre-heated oven (375°/190°C) for ± 15-20 minutes or until the cheese is melted and light golden-brown.

Serve as main or side dish.

Potato *Gratin* d'Provence

Serves 2

Who doesn't love a good potato dish?

Ingredients:

- 2 large potatoes, peeled, sliced thin • ½ cup bacon pieces, crisped in the oven
- 1 cup grated young cheese, like Edam or Beemster® Vlaskaas cheese
- 2 Tablespoons Herbs d' Provence • 2 Tablespoons cream • Salt & pepper tt

  1 - Place a layer of potato slices in an oven-safe dish. Pour a little cream over the potato slices. Sprinkle with bacon pieces, grated cheese, Herbs d 'Provence and a little salt and pepper.

  2 - Repeat this until potato slices are used up, and finish with grated cheese and a few bacon pieces.

  3 - Place, covered with aluminum foil, in a pre-heated oven (375°/190°C) for ± 20-25 minutes. Uncover and return to oven for an additional 5 minutes until slightly golden brown.

Beans & *Cheese* Salad

Serves 4

An easy to prepare salad filled with heart-healthy fiber: beans, barley, bell pepper prepared to satisfaction with a little turkey bacon and cheese.

Ingredients Beans & Cheese Salad:

- 2 cups Goya 16 bean mix, soaked overnight
- 1 Ready Pac® bell pepper mix
- ½ cup canned or frozen corn kernels
- 1 cup pearl barley
- ¼ cup turkey bacon strips, crisped in the oven, drained, cut into strips
- 1 cup young cheese, like Beemster® Vlaskaas, cut into small cubes
- Salt & pepper to taste
- 1 teaspoon Tabasco® hot-sauce
- Chives for garnish

1 - Place the soaked beans in a pan with enough water to cover them. Bring to a boil and let simmer for ± 2 hours or until 'Al Dente' (tender to bite).

2 - Place barley in a pan with 1 cup water. Bring to a boil, and let simmer for ± 45 minutes or until tender.

3 - Combine ingredients and, chill for ± ½ hour minimum in the refrigerator.

4 - Serve with a bowl of sunflower seeds, cilantro leaves and a garlic/yogurt dressing.

Ingredients garlic/yogurt dressing:

- 2 cups plain yogurt
- 2 Tablespoons garlic, minced
- 1/3 cup chopped fresh mint
- Pinch salt & pepper to taste

1 - Mix ingredients, and serve on the side.

15

Scandinavian Smoked *Salmon* Roses

Serves 10

Beautiful, mouth watering appetizers to make your party a great success.
Ingredients:
- 10 Fillo dough cups, at room temperature
- 4 oz. smoked salmon, cut into ½ inch strips • ⅓ cup whipped cream
- 3 Tablespoons grated Beemster® Classic cheese • ¼ cup onion, chopped
- ¼ cup apple, small diced • 2 Tablespoons coarse mustard
- Coarse ground black pepper • 10 dill plushes for garnish

1 - Mix cream, cheese, onion, apple, and mustard.
    Season with a little salt and pepper.
2 - Cut salmon into strips and roll them into the shape of a rose.
3 - Divide the cream mixture over the 10 fillo dough cups.
4 - Garnish with a dill plush and sprinkle with black pepper.

Creamy *Wonton* Triangles

Serves 10

Ingredients:
- 10 wonton squares • 8 oz. cream cheese, softened • ¼ cup onion, chopped finely • 1 Tablespoon low-sodium soy sauce • 1/2 cup sesame oil • 10 cilantro plushes for garnish • ground black pepper

1 - Mix cream cheese, onion, and soy sauce into a smooth mixture.
2 - Place 1 Tablespoon of the mixture in the center of each wonton.
3 - Fold 2 edges together. Press edges.
4 - Heat sesame oil, and fry triangles on each side for 30 seconds.
4 - Garnish with fig chutney (page 73), a cilantro plush and serve warm.

Party *Cheese* Shapes

Serves 10

Ingredients:
- ½ lb. cheese of choice, cut into ½ inch slices
- 2 Tablespoons chunky, fig-chutney (page 73) • 10 cilantro plushes for garnish

1 - Cut cheese into flowers or other fun shapes and garnish with ½ teaspoon fig puree and a cilantro plush.

Ham & *Cheese* Profiterole

Ingredients profiterole:

- 1 cup water • 1 cup all-purpose flour
- ¾ stick / 6 Tablespoons unsalted butter • 1 teaspoon salt • 4 eggs

    1 - Pre-heat oven to 400°F/205°C. Spray a baking sheet with a little oil.

    2 - Place butter, water and salt in a saucepan. Bring to a boil.

    3 - Add the flour, and stir constantly with a wooden or silicone spoon until the mixture becomes a ball. Remove from the stove and let cool for a few minutes, before adding eggs, one at a time.

    4 - Use a pastry bag with a large tip to pipe small, teaspoon size, balls onto the baking sheet, leaving at least 2 inches space in between.

    5 - Bake for 10 minutes, then reduce heat to 350°F/175°C, and bake for another 15-20 minutes, until light golden brown.

Ingredients filling:

- 1 Tablespoon butter • 1 Tablespoon flour • 1/3 cup ham, small diced
- 1 cup grated cheese • ½ cup Creme Fraiche

    1 - Melt butter, and flour. Stir for 1 minute. Add rest of the ingredients. Use a pastry bag with a large tip to fill the profiteroles.

TIP: This filling also tastes great on a pumpernickel or wheat toast. Use a pastry bag with a star tip and garnish with a small parsley plush.

Fruit & *Cheese* Kebab

A colorful snack, appetizer, or party item with a fusion of flavors and textures. You can create any combination with fruits, cherry tomatoes, olives and any kind of cheese with different ages and flavors.

Example ingredients per kebab:

- 1 strawberry, a cube of Beemster® garlic cheese, 1 grape, a cube of a mature cheese, 1 kiwi, 1 cube of young cheese, 1 cube of melon.

    1 - Assemble the kebabs and stick them in a orange, covered with aluminum foil to make a beautiful presentation.

Mandarin & *Cheese* Salad

Serves 4

Salads are the most diverse gifts of Mother Nature with unlimited possible flavor and texture combinations.

Ingredients:

- 8 oz. mixed greens, washed, dried
- 1 cup young cheese, like Beemster® Vlaskaas, cut into small cubes
- 1 cup mandarin or orange segments
- 2 Tablespoons almond sliced, toasted
- ½ cup fresh herbs: thyme, oregano, basil

1 - Dry-roast the almond slices in a non-stick pan for 2-3 minutes.

2 - Cut ingredients into desired sizes.

3 - Divide ingredients over 4 plates, and serve with dressing on the side.

Ingredients dressing:

- ¼ extra virgin olive oil • ½ cup balsamic vinegar
- 1 teaspoon dried basil • 1 Tablespoon garlic, minced
- Fresh ground black pepper

1 - Mix all ingredients.

Fresh fruit and nuts in main-dish recipes are a great way to add health benefits to your food. Nuts are high in vitamin E, a very important anti-oxidant, which helps reduce the risk of heart disease and cancer. Nuts, especially almonds, hazelnuts and walnuts, contain unsaturated fats and omega 3s, which help lower bad cholesterol, plus nuts are a great source of protein and fiber.
Of course, if you have to watch your weight, you also should limit your calorie intake, and nuts are high in calories. A small handful of nuts a day gives you all the health benefits, and you limit the calories.

Salmon & *Cheese* Lasagna

Serves 2

Ingredients:

- 12 lasagna sheets, 2 x 4 inch
- Sauce: 1 cup cream combined with ½ cup tomato sauce, 2 tablespoons vodka, and salt & pepper to taste
- 16 slices plus ⅓ cup grated cheese of choice
- 6-8 oz salmon, sliced into ¼ inch thick slices
- 1 cup bell pepper mix, chopped
- 3 Tablespoons capers
- 3 Tablespoons pine nuts
- 1 cup basil leaves
- 1 zucchini, sliced

1 - Pre-heat oven to 375°F/190°C.

2 - Scoop a spoonful of the sauce onto the bottom of an oven-safe dish. Place 4 lasagna sheets on top of the sauce.

3 - Assemble: 1 layer of ⅓ of each: cheese, salmon slices, bell pepper, pinenuts, capers, basil, zucchini, sauce and 4 sheets of lasagna.

4 - Repeat the same order of assembly twice, finishing with grated cheese on top of the last layer of lasagna sheets.

5 - Place in the oven and bake for ± 30-35 minutes.

Colorful *Chèvre* Potato Salad

Serves 2-4

Chèvre cheese is made from goat's milk (chèvre is French for goat). Goat cheese is whiter in color, and available is soft, semi-hard and hard. For this recipe we choose the Goat Gouda. It is tangy, satiny, mouth-watering cheese, and a firm body, but not hard enough to grate.

Ingredients salad:

- 1 teaspoon butter • 1 shallot, finely chopped • 1 teaspoon garlic, minced
- 4 cups red skin potato, cut into cubes, cooked, chilled
- 2 Tablespoons red bell pepper, chopped
- 1 cup Dutch goat cheese, cut into small cubes • Salt & pepper to taste
    1 - Heat butter until melted, not browned. Add shallot and garlic. Stir until translucent.
    2 - In a large bowl, mix all ingredients and season with a little sea salt and pepper. Chill for ± 30 minutes. Serve with honey dressing on the side.

Refreshing *Chèvre* & Pear Salad

Serves 2-4

Refreshing, and bold are the two main characteristics of this simple to make salad.

Ingredients salad:

- 1 cup Dutch goat cheese, cut into small cubes • 4 cups Frisee & Arugala lettuce
- 1 pear, cored and sliced thin
    1 - Cut ingredients to desired shapes.
    2 - In a large bowl, mix all ingredients and serve with dressing on the side.

Ingredients honey dressing:

- 2 Tablespoons extra virgin olive oil • ½ Tablespoon white wine vinegar
- 1 Tablespoon honey • 1 teaspoon fresh thyme or ½ teaspoon dried
- A little sea salt & pepper to taste

Spinach & *Cheese* Meatloaf

Serves 4

The comfort of home cooking fills your kitchen with delightful fragrances, and this dish keeps bringing back memories of cozy family dinners. For this recipe, we used a "Boerenkaas"- farmers cheese. Boerenkaas is only made from May to October when the cows can stay outside and eat fresh grass. Made from raw milk and aged for six months to assure a full, tangy, and bold flavor.

Ingredients:

- 1 Tablespoon olive oil
- 1 cup onion, chopped
- ¼ cup pinenuts
- 2 cups spinach, coarsely chopped
- 1 ½ lbs. ground turkey
- 2 eggs
- 1 cup breadcrumbs
- 1 ½ cups Boerenkaas of other bold flavored cheese of choice, sliced or grated
- Salt & pepper to taste

1 - Pre-heat oven to 375°F/190°C.

2 - Place oil in the skillet. Sauté the onions and pinenuts until onions are lightly caramelized.

3 - Add spinach, stir for about 2 minutes, until slightly wilted.

4 - Place ground turkey in a large bowl, and season with a little salt and pepper. Add egg and breadcrumbs. Mix well.

5 - Place ⅓ of the meat into an oven-safe dish, top with ⅓ of the onion/spinach mixture, and ⅓ cup of the cheese.

6 - Repeat this twice, finishing with the cheese and place the dish in pre-heated oven for 25-30 minutes. Pour off excess liquid, if needed.

7 - Serve warm with mashed or roasted potatoes and a little gravy.

Deep Dish *Cheese & Veggie* Pie

Serves 6-8

Satisfaction is guaranteed with this delicious combination of Mother Nature's gifts. The recipe gives a lot of room for creativity of the cook; add ingredients; change flavors, any combinations will be just mouth-watering!

Ingredients:

- 2 cups mushrooms, sliced
- 2 cups spinach, washed, drained
- 2 cups bell pepper mix
- 1 cup cherry tomatoes
- 1 cup broccoli florets
- 4 cups Eggbeaters
- $\frac{1}{8}$ cup light cream or H&H
- 1 cup 'Belegen' matured cheese, like a mature Gouda or Beemster® Classic cheese, grated
- Salt & pepper to taste
- 2 teaspoons Herbs d'Provence
- Curled parsley for garnish

1 - Pre-heat oven to 375°F/190°C.

2 - Line the spring form with plastic wrap, overlapping in the middle and hanging over the sides.

3 - Arrange a layer of mushrooms to cover the bottom, followed by a layer of spinach, bell pepper, cherry tomatoes, broccoli and cheese.

4 - Repeat this and finish with the broccoli.

5 - Mix eggbeaters with cream, Herbs d'Provence, and season with a little salt and pepper. Pour over the layers.

6 - Add last layer of cheese and place in oven for ± 1 hour until set in the center.

Extravagant Pasta

Serves 4

A rich, delicious pasta loaded with seafood and finished with the enigmatic flavor of Beemster® Nettle cheese.

Ingredients Extravagant & Seafood Pasta:

- 1 Tablespoon olive oil • 1 Tablespoon garlic, minced
- 2 Tablespoons shallot, minced • ½ cup leek, sliced thin • 1 bay leaf
- 2 cups fish or vegetable stock • 1 cup white wine • 1 cup scallops
- 1 cup shrimp, peeled and deveined • 1 cup crawfish
- 1 cup New Zealand mussels (removed from shells following package instructions) • 1 lobster tail, cut into bite-size pieces
- ½ cup light cream or H&H
- Salt & pepper to taste
- Slurry: 1 Tablespoon arrowroot mixed with 1 Tablespoon water
- Pasta of choice
- ½ cup Beemster® Nettle cheese, cut into small cubes
- 1 Tablespoon parsley, finely chopped

1 - Heat large pan, add olive oil. Add garlic, shallot, and stir around until translucent.

2 - Add bay leaf, leek, stock, wine, and cream, bring to a boil.

3 - Add scallops, shrimp, mussels, crawfish, and lobster tail pieces.

4 - Season with a little salt and pepper. Add slurry.
Let simmer for 10 - 15 minutes, and meanwhile start pasta (see 5).

5 - Boil water and add pasta, boil for amount of minutes stated on the package.

6 - Mix drained pasta with seafood mixture, stir around for 1 minute, garnish with a little grated cheese and parsley.

Delft Blue *Cheese* Chicken Oven Dish

Serves 4

Delft Blue is the famous china from the little town Delft in Holland. The Delft Blue cheese is a blue and white cheese made of cow milk with a rich and creamy, slightly buttery, mellow taste and a clean finish.

Ingredients:

- 12 chicken drum sticks
- 3 Tablespoons breadcrumbs
- 1 Tablespoon Italian seasoning: rosemary, thyme, oregano
- 3 cups tomato, diced
- 1 cup blue cheese, like the Dutch Delft Blue, crumbled + 1 Tablespoon for each plate
- Salt & pepper to taste
- 4 Tablespoons mushrooms of choice or a mix of various types, chopped
- 2 Tablespoons butter
- 1 cup spaghetti, cooked

1 - Pre-heat oven to 375°F/190°C. Mix salt, pepper, Italian seasoning, breadcrumbs.

2 - Rub the drums with the breadcrumb mix.

3 - Place diced tomato at the bottom of an oven-safe dish. Add drums.

4 - Place in the pre-heated oven for ± 45 minutes.

5 - Remove dish from oven. Divide cup of blue cheese over the drums, and return to the oven for an additional 10 minutes,

6 - In the mean time, heat skillet with butter. Add mushrooms, garlic and a little salt and pepper. Stir around for about 5 minutes.

7 - While working on mushrooms and chicken, bring enough water to a boil for the spaghetti. Boil spaghetti according to the instructions on the package.

8 - Assembly: Place 1/4 of the drained spaghetti in the center of the plate. Top this with 1/4 of the tomato mixture, and place 3 drums in the center of the spaghetti.

Place 1 Tablespoon of blue cheese on one side and 1 Tablespoon of the mushroom mixture on the other side.

Shrimp & *Cheese* Stuffed Hot Peppers

Serves 4

Southern flavors are bold, honest flavors. Seafood combined with spicy ingredients and comforting cheese..... just yummy!

Ingredients Shrimp & Cheese Stingers:
- 8 jumbo jalapeños or long hot peppers
- 1 cup Beemster® garlic cheese, small diced or shredded
- 1 cup shrimp, peeled, deveined, chopped • 1 Tablespoon shallot, minced
- 1 Tablespoon bacon, crisped in the oven or packaged ready-to-serve, chopped • Salt & pepper to taste

1 - Slice hot pepper in half, remove seeds, to make it less hot.
2 - Mix shrimp, cheese, shallot, bacon and season with a little salt and pepper.
3 - Stuff hot pepper with the shrimp mixture.
4 - Place in pre-heated oven (375°F/190°C) for 20 minutes.
5 - Serve warm.

Onion, Garlic & *Cheese* Scones

Serves 4

A snack, small lunch.... it is smelly and delicious!

Ingredients:
- 1 ½ cups all-purpose flour • 2 teaspoons baking powder
- ½ cup onion, finely chopped • 1 Tablespoon garlic, minced
- 1 cup mature cheese, like Beemster® Classic Cheese, grated
- ½ teaspoon salt • ¾ cup milk • 1 large egg

1 - Pre-heat oven to 375°F/190°C. Spray a little oil on cookie sheet.
2 - In a bowl, mix flour, baking powder, onion, garlic, cheese, salt, egg and milk.
3 - Place 3 Tablespoons of the mixture on the cookie sheet, and place in pre-heated oven for 15-20 minutes, or until golden brown.

Gorgeous & Delicious  Tower

Party center piece

> *A beautiful center piece for every party: a delicious, rich cheese tower. The dividers are made of Beemster® XO cheese following the recipe on page 73, one plain, one with poppy seeds added and one with sesame seeds added.*

Ingredients Cheese Tower:

- 8 oz cream cheese, softened
- 1 bunch chives, chopped
- 1 cup grated cheese of choice
- 1 Tablespoon caviar
- 3 blossoms chives or other high-green garnish
- 1 Tablespoon prickly pear sauce for decorative dots (see page 71)

1 - Assemble: Place 1 nutty tuille in the center of your plate or platter.

2 - Roll ½ of the cream cheese into the shape of a ball, and roll it through the chopped chives. Place it in the center of the tuille cookie.

3 - Place the next tuille divider on top of the chive-cheese ball.

4 - Roll the other ½ of the cream cheese into the shape of a ball, and roll it through the grated cheese. Place it in the center of the tuille cookie.

5 - Carefully make a small hole in the center of the top tuille cookie and place the cookie on top of the grated cheese-cream cheese ball.

6 - Place your blossom chives into the hole, or if you need to stabilize the tower, add a (decorative) skewer in the center first.

7 - Decorate your plate with the prickly pear sauce dots.

8 - Serve with crackers and small toast.

Spicy Sausage & *Cheese* Flatbread

Serves 4-6

Sausages are available in a wide variety: mild Italian, spicy Italian, but also stuffed with chicken, turkey, herbs, cheeses, tomato and spinach. We used the spicy Italian for this recipe, but you can use any kind of sausage.

Ingredients:
- 1 Tablespoon olive oil • ½ cup onion, chopped
- 4 spicy Italian sausages, cut into ½ inch pieces
- 1 cup mushrooms, sliced • 1 cup bell pepper mix, chopped
- ¼ cup olives, pits removed, sliced • 1 Tablespoon sun-dried tomato, sliced
- 1 cup grated beautiful spiced cheese, like Beemster® Mustard cheese
- Salt & pepper to taste • 1 Tablespoon Italian herb mix
- 1 store bought pizza dough ball, or see recipe
- ½ cup basil leaves, cut into a chiffonade (rolled up, cut into strips)

1 - Pre-heat oven to 375°F/190°C.
2 - Place 1 Tablespoon oil in the skillet. Add sausage pieces and onion until lightly caramelized.
3 - Roll, stretch dough to a flat circle or square (depending on shape of baking sheet or stone).
4 - Divide mushroom slices, bell pepper, olive slices, and sun-dried tomato slices over the dough and sprinkle with a little salt, pepper, and Italian herb mix.
4 - Add sausage pieces, onion mix, and grated cheese.
5 - Place in the oven for ± 20 minutes or until crust is light golden brown.
6 - Garnish with a basil chiffonade and serve warm.

Ingredients - whole wheat pizza dough:
- 1 package dry yeast • 1 cup warm water
- 1 Tablespoon honey
- 3 cups whole wheat flour

1 - Let yeast dissolve in the warm water.
2 - Add honey, stir and allow to stand a few minutes.
3 - Place all ingredients in a mixer bowl and knead to form a dough.
4 - Place in lightly oiled bowl. Cover and let rise about 45 minutes.
5 - Punch down, roll, stretch dough to a flat circle or square (depending on shape of baking sheet or stone).

Scrumptious  Cobb Salad

Serves 2

The Cobb Salad was invented in 1928 in Los Angeles. It is a salad loaded with bold flavors and exciting textures.

Ingredients Scrumptious Cobb Salad:

- 2 cups mixed lettuce
- 1 cup grilled chicken breast, cut into bite size pieces
- 2 slices bacon, crisped in the oven, coarsely chopped
- ½ avocado, sliced
- 1 cup cherry tomatoes
- ½ cup blue cheese, crumbled, like Delft Blue cheese
- 2 hard boiled eggs, sliced
- 1 Tablespoon Herb d'Provence
- Fresh ground black pepper to taste

1 - Assemble ingredients on 2 plates.

2 - Serve with dressing on the side.

Ingredients Dressing:

- ½ cup blue cheese, crumbled, like Delft Blue cheese
- ¼ cup Champagne or white wine vinegar
- ½ cup buttermilk
- 1 Tablespoon shallots, minced
- 1 Tablespoon fresh parsley, minced or 1 Tablespoon dried parsley
- 1 teaspoon Worcestershire sauce
- ½ teaspoon garlic, minced

1 - Mix all ingredients. Stays fresh refrigerated for ± 1 week.

Zucchini, Beef & *Cheese*

Carpaccio

Serves 4

Bold flavors will satisfy your appetite and keep your taste buds interested.

Ingredients Carpaccio:

- 4 zucchini, sliced thin using slicer, center with seeds discarded
- 1 Tablespoon olive oil
- 2 teaspoons garlic, minced
- 2 Tablespoons shallots, sliced thin
- 1 cup mushrooms, sliced
- 2 Tablespoons pinenuts, roasted
- ½ pound rare roast beef, very thin sliced
- 1 cup Frisee lettuce
- ¼ cup very old cheese, like Beemster® XO cheese, shaved
- Flor de Sal (purest sea salt)

1 - Place zucchini in heated pan with a little olive oil on each side for 1 minute or grill for 1 minute on each side.
    Drain on paper towel and divide the zucchini slices and ¼ of the roast beef slices over 4 plates.

2 - Add shallot, garlic and mushroom to the pan. Stir occasionally until lightly caramelized.

3 - Divide mixture over the 4 plates. Roast pinenuts in a dry, non-stick pan for 1 minute.

4 - Garnish with ¼ cup Frisee in the center, with ½ Tablespoon toasted pinenuts and a little XO cheese on top.

5 - Sprinkle with dressing and a little Flor de Sal.

TIP: This recipe is also great with a bold flavored blue cheese, like Delft Blue or a Trappist Blue Cheese

Dressing:

- 3 Tablespoons Balsamic vinegar
- ½ cup extra virgin olive oil
- 1 teaspoon Italian seasoning (dried basil, oregano, thyme, rosemary)

Tuna, Eggplant & Frittata

Serves 6-8

Bold flavors are beautifully combined in this simple frittata.

Ingredients tuna, eggplant & cheese frittata:

- 1 Tablespoon olive oil
- 6 scallions, sliced
- 1 cup eggplant, small diced
- 1 Tablespoon capers
- ½ Tablespoon garlic, minced
- 6 oz (1 can) tuna in water, drained, loosened with a fork
- 1 cup of cheese of choice, grated or small diced
- 8 oz eggbeaters® or 4 eggs, beaten with 1 Tablespoon of skim milk
- Salt & pepper to taste
- Frisee lettuce sprigs for garnish

1 - Pre-heat oven to 375°F/190°C.
2 - Place 1 Tablespoon oil in an oven-safe skillet. Sauté the onion until lightly caramelized.
3 - Add eggplant, garlic, capers and a pinch of sea salt and pepper. Stir around for 2 minutes.
4 - Add tuna to the skillet. Stir around to mix, and pour eggs or eggbeaters® over the mixture. Sprinkle cheese on top.
5 - Place skillet in the pre-heated oven for ± 20-30 minutes until set in the center.
6 - Garnish with a sprig of Frisee lettuce, and serve warm with a piece of hearty, whole wheat or multi grain bread.

Various Mini *Cheese* Sandwich Triangles

Serves 4 per recipe

Small wheat, white, and rye sandwiches with a variety of toppings are called canapes. Be creative with items and presentation.

Ingredients Smoked Salmon canapes:

- 8 slices wheat bread, crust removed (optional, crust is great fiber source)
- 4 oz smoked salmon, cut into ½ inch high strips
- 8 slices of cheese of choice
- 1 Tablespoon Devon Double Cream • 1 Tablespoon yogurt
- 2 Tablespoons onion, chopped • ¼ apple, cored, sliced thin
- 1 Tablespoon coarse mustard • Coarse ground black pepper
    1 - Mix Devon Double Cream, onion, apple, mustard, cheese and yogurt. Season with a little salt and pepper.
    2 - Divide the cream mixture over 4 slices of bread.
    3 - Assemble: 1 slice of bread with cream mixture, 1 slice of smoked salmon, a few slices of apple, and top with another slice of bread.

Ingredients Cheese Tuna Melt canapes:

- 4 rye or pumpernickel bread slices
- 4 lettuce leaves, washed and dried
- 8 oz tuna (in water), drained, loosened with a fork, mixed with 1 Tablespoon mayonnaise and ½ teaspoon lemon juice
- 1 tomato, sliced
- 8 slices young cheese, like a Beemster® Vlaskaas
    1 - Assemble: 1 slice of bread, 1 lettuce leaf, 2 oz tuna, 1 slice tomato, 2 slices cheese.
    2 - Place under broiler for 2-3 minutes, until cheese is melted.

Ingredients Beemster® Garlic cheese with Roast Beef canapes:

- 8 slices country bread
- 8 slices cheese • 4 slices roast beef • 2 Tablespoons coarse mustard
    1 - Assemble: 2 slices of bread, 2 slices cheese and 1 slice of roast beef

For a fun presentation, you can use skewers to make a bread kebab, or place the triangles on a platter with some lettuce or colorful cabbage with cherry tomatoes and grapes as decoration.

47

Surprising *Cheese* Pouches

Serves 4

A side dish or snack with a rich-flavor surprise inside.

Ingredients Cheese Pouch 1:

- 2 slices ham, ¼ inch thick, diced
- 1 cup grated young cheese, like Beemster® Vlaskaas cheese
- 2 Tablespoons white wine • 1 Tablespoon cream
- Salt & pepper to taste • 1 Tablespoon parsley, chopped

1 - Place ham in the skillet. Stir for 1 minute.

2 - Add cheese, white wine, cream, season with a little salt and pepper, and chopped parsley. Stir around for 1 minute.

3 - Spoon 2 Tablespoons of the mixture onto the center of the crepes, fold crepes into the shape of a bag, and secure with a chive, or ribbon cut from a green onion or leek green.

Ingredients Cheese Pouch 2:

- 2 slices salami, ¼ inch thick, diced
- ½ cup grated mature cheese, like Beemster® Classic cheese
- ¼ cup tomato, diced • 1 Tablespoon tomato ketchup
- Salt & pepper to taste • 1 Tablespoon oregano, chopped

1 - Place salami and tomato dices in the skillet. Stir for 1 minute.

2 - Add cheese, ketchup, season with a little salt and pepper, and chopped oregano. Stir around for 1 minute.

3 - Spoon 2 Tablespoons of the mixture onto the center of the crepes, fold crepes into the shape of a bag, and secure with a chive, or ribbon cut from a green onion or leek green.

Ingredients crepes:

- 1 ½ cups all-purpose flour • 1 Tablespoon sugar
- 1 teaspoon salt • 3 eggs
- ½ cup milk • 2 Tablespoons neutral oil (avocado - canola)

1 - Mix all ingredients using an electric mixer.

2 - Set aside for ± 30 minutes before making the crepes.

Beemster® Vlaskaas  Cheese Fondue

Serves 4-6

A center piece on your party table or a cozy family evening, a Beemster® cheese fondue is always a hit.

Ingredients:
- 2 Tablespoons butter
- 2 Tablespoons flour
- 2 ½ cups of Vlaskaas, cut into cubes or grated
- 1 cup white wine
- 2 cups of half and half or 2% milk
- Pinch of sea salt and white pepper

1 - Heat a thick bottomed pan, and let butter melt.

2 - Add flour, bring to a boil, and stir around for 1-2 minutes.

3 - Take pan from the stove, and gradually add milk and wine, stirring until mixture is smooth, and season with a little salt and pepper.

4 - Bring to a boil, and let simmer for 2-3 minutes.

5 - Take pan from the stove, and gradually add Vlaskaas, stirring until mixture is smooth.

6 - Pour into the fondue pan.

Dipping items:
- 2 cups small red-skin potatoes, boiled for 2 minutes, cut in half
- 1 cup shrimp, peeled and deveined, boiled for 1 minute
- 1 cup lobster tail, peeled, cut into 1 inch pieces, boiled for 2 minutes
- 5 slices of country bread/French bread, toasted, cut into cubes or shapes
- 1 cup asparagus, cut into 1 inch pieces, boiled for 1 minute
- 1 cup broccoli florets
- 1 cup cherry tomatoes

Colorful Macaroni & *Cheese* with Tomato Sauce

Serves 4

Ingredients Colorful Macaroni:

- 2 cups macaroni, cooked • 1 Tablespoon olive oil
- 1 shallot, sliced • 1 Tablespoon garlic
- 1 cup bell pepper mix (orange, green, red), chopped
- Salt & pepper to taste • 1 Tablespoon parsley, chopped finely for garnish
- ½ cup grated young cheese, like Beemster® Vlaskaas

  1 - Heat pan, add oil and sauté onion and garlic until translucent. Add bell pepper mix; stir around for ± 3 minutes. Season with a little salt and pepper to taste.

  2 - Boil macaroni according to instructions on package. Drain and add to bell pepper mix. Stir around for 1 minute.

  3 - Garnish macaroni dish with parsley and grated cheese.

Ingredients Tomato Sauce:

- ½ cup H&H or light cream • 1 cup tomato sauce
- 1 teaspoon hot sauce • Salt & pepper to taste

  1 - In a saucepan, heat tomato sauce with cream and season to taste with a little sea salt, black pepper, and hot sauce.

  2 - Serve with sauce on the side.

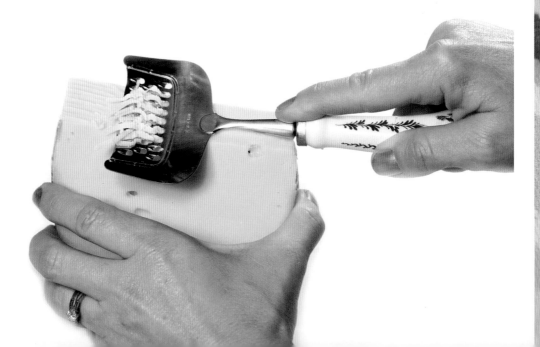

Impressionable *Oyster* Gratin

Serves 4

Seafood, especially oysters, scallops, shrimp and lobster are known for their love enhancing powers. These receipes are light, delightful, and even mood enhancing. This oyster recipe is an excellent dinner for a romantic date.

Ingredients:

- 10 oysters • 1 Tablespoon garlic, minced • 1 Tablespoon white wine
- 1 Tablespoon oregano or ½ Tablespoon dried oregano
- ½ cup mature cheese, like a Beemster® Classic cheese, grated
- 1 Tablespoon black caviar as garnish

  1 - Preheat oven to 375°F/190°C. Open the oysters with a special oyster knife, wearing an anti-cutting glove. Discard the flat oyster shell. Loosen the oyster from the bottom shell. Rinse both well.

  2 - Heat white wine, garlic, oregano and poach oysters ± 1 minute. Place each oyster on a bottom shell and cover them with a tablespoon grated cheese.

  3 - Place under the broiler or in a pre-heated oven for ± 2 minutes.

  4 - Garnish with ½ teaspoon of caviar on each oyster gratin.

Pairing Wine

A wine can have echelon of black current, blackberries, raspberries, sweet oak or a range of other flavors. All the gorgeous vineyards in the world have their own romance and style of making wine. And, how do you pair wine with cheese?

A few simple guidelines. A strong cheese needs a bold wine.

Hard cheeses	Red wine
Soft cheeses	White wine, Vinho Verde (Portuguese green wine), Gewurztraminer, Champagne
Blue cheese and goat cheese	Beaujolais, Bordeaux, Cabernet, Port

A little more detailed:

Cheddar, strong	Merlot, Cabernet Sauvignon, Shirah, Red Zinfandel
Cheddar, mild	Cabernet Blanc, Pinot Blanc, Pinot Grigio, Zinfandel
Gouda, young	Beaujolais, Pinot Grigio, Riesling, Champagne
Beemster® XO and Classic	Merlot, Cabernet Sauvignon, Shirah, Red Zinfandel

Belgian Beer & *Cheese*

Stew

Serves 4

A rich flavored stew loaded with vegetables, flavored with Belgian beer and Beemster® Vlaskaas is a great meal for a cosy evening at home.
Ingredients:

- 1 pound beef rump or chuck roast, cut into cubes
- 1 Tablespoon olive or vegetable oil
- ½ pound onions, thinly sliced • 1 cup carrots, sliced • 1 cup celery, sliced
- 4 medium or 8 small red-skin potatoes, quarted
- 2 slices smoked ham, diced • 1 cup mushrooms, sliced
- 2 cups beef broth • 1 pint Belgian beer
- 1 bay leaf • 1 teaspoon sugar • 2 teaspoons salt
- 1 bouquet garni: greens of celery, leek, thyme, or parsley, (tied together)
- 2 teaspoons fresh ground black pepper
- 1 cup of young cheese of choice, like a Beemster® Vlaskaas or a young Gouda, cut into small cubes • 3 Tablespoons parsley, chopped

1 - Cut meat into cubes. Heat pan with a little oil and brown meat on all sides.

2 - Add onions until light golden. Add carrots, celery, potatoes, ham, mushrooms, broth, beer, bay leaf, sugar, salt, bouquet garni, and pepper.

3 - Bring to a boil and let simmer for 2 to 2 ½ hours until meat is tender. Add more beer or stock, if needed.

4 - Add cheese and garnish with parsley.

5 - Serve with fresh country bread and glass of Belgian beer.

Spinach &  *Cheese* Soup

Serves 4-6

Ingredients:

- ½ cup bacon, cut into strips • 1 onion, finely chopped
- 1 Tablespoon garlic, minced • 1 pint vegetable stock • 3 saffron threads
- 2 cups potato, peeled, washed, cut in ¼" cubes • 1 cup cream or H&H • 2 cups spinach • ½ cup grated young cheese • Salt & pepper to taste

1 - Heat pan, add bacon, garlic and onion, stir around until golden brown and bacon is crisp. Using a slotted spoon, remove bacon mixture from the pan, set aside, and pour grease out of the pan.

2 - Add stock, saffron and potato cubes, bring to a boil, and let simmer for 10-15 minutes, stirring occasionally.

3 - Add spinach and grated cheese, and let simmer for an additional 2 minutes. Using a slotted spoon, place mixture in blender, and blend until smooth.

4 - Return all ingredients to the pan. Add cream, and a little salt and pepper. Let simmer for additional 2 minutes.

Red Lentil &  *Cheese* Soup

Serves 4-6

Ingredients:

- 1 Tablespoon butter • 1 Tablespoon garlic, minced • 1 shallot, minced
- 1 cup celery, small diced • 1 cup carrot, shredded • 1 cup bell pepper mix, chopped • 1 pint vegetable stock • 2 cups red lentils
- 1 Tablespoon curry powder • 1 teaspoon cumin • ½ cup H&H
- ¼ cup grated young mature cheese • Salt & pepper to taste

1 - Heat butter in a skillet. Add garlic and shallot, stir until translucent.

2 - Add celery, carrot, bell pepper and stir for an additional minute.

3 - Add stock, lentils, curry powder and cumin, bring to a boil, and let simmer for 20-25 minutes, stirring occasionally until lentils are tender.

4 - Add H&H, grated cheese, and season with a little salt and pepper.

5 - Bring to a boil and let simmer for an additional minute.

Garnish with a cheese tuille (see page 73).

Delicious *Cheese* Panini

Serves 2

The name of a warm sandwich is 'Tosti' (Germany-Holland), 'Panini' in Italy, "Croque Monsieur" or "Croque Madame - tosti with fried egg on top" in France.

Ingredients Panini 1:

- 4 slices wheat or multi-grain bread
- 4 slices eggplant (use peeler to slice thin)
- 6 slices tomato
- 6 slices herb flavored cheese, like Beemster® Nettle cheese
- A little "Flor de Sal" and black pepper

1 - Pre-heat panini maker or George Foreman Grill.

2 - Grill or sauté eggplant slices for 1 minute on each side.

3 - Assemble each panini: 1 slice of bread, 2 eggplant slices, sprinkle with a little 'Flor de Sal" and fresh ground black pepper, 3 tomato slices, 3 cheese slices, 1 slice of bread.

4 - Place in panini maker or GF-grill for ± 2-3 minutes, until cheese has melted and bread is light golden brown.

5 - Serve with cold glass of milk.

Ingredients Panini 2:

- 4 slices Mediterranean cheese bread (see page 65)
- 4 slices zucchini (use peeler to slice thin)
- 4 slices turkey breast (deli)
- 4 slices mature cheese, like a Beemster® Classic cheese
- 1 Tablespoon coarse mustard
- Basil leaves

1 - Pre-heat panini maker or George Foreman Grill.

2 - Grill or sautée zucchini slices for 1 minute on each side.

3 - Assemble each panini: 1 slice of bread, mustard, 2 zucchini slices, 2 turkey breast slices, 2 cheese slices, 1 slice of bread.

4 - Place in panini maker or GF-grill for ± 2-3 minutes, until cheese has melted and bread is light golden brown.

Three  Cheese Ravioli

Makes 16

Ravioli is fun to make. The easiest way is to use a pasta maker, but a rolling pin also does the job. Ravioli can be served as an appetizer, lunch, or dinner.

Ingredients Ravioli dough:
- 2 cups unbleached flour • 1 cup wheat flour
- 4 eggs • 2 egg yolks • pinch sea salt • pinch nutmeg

    1 - Mix dough. Roll out with rolling pin to $\frac{1}{8}$" thickness. Cut squares.

Ingredients 3 Cheese Ravioli filling:
- 12 slices old cheese, like a Beemster ® XO cheese
- 12 slices Beemster® Mustard cheese
- 12 slices blue cheese, like Delft Blue

    1 - Add 1 slice cheese folded square, slightly smaller than the dough, into the center of the ravioli square. Use cheese slicer for even thickness.

    2 - Brush edges of dough with a damp brush, and add top dough square.

    3 - Press edges together with your fingers or a fork.

    4 - Boil raviolis for 8-10 minutes.

Ingredients Lobster-Vodka-Tomato Cream Sauce:
- 2 lobster tails, removed from shell and cut into small pieces. Save tail for garnishing
- 1 Tablespoon olive oil • 1 shallot, finely chopped • ½ cup vodka
- 1 cup H&H or light cream • 1 Tablespoon tomato paste
- 6 basil leaves, chiffonade (cut into thin strips) • sea salt and pepper to taste

    1 - Heat olive oil in skillet. Add shallot, stir around until translucent.

    2 - Add vodka, cream and tomato paste. Stir until smooth. Add a little sea salt and pepper to taste.

    3 - Add lobster and bring to a boil, and let simmer for 8-10 minutes.

    4 - Add basil chiffonade just before serving.

Whole Wheat &  Cheese Bread Delights

Bread and cheese are a great combination. Imagine cheese in bread, the delicious, rich flavor of cheese in every bite.

Ingredients Whole Wheat dough:

- 2 cups whole wheat flour • 1 cup bread flour • 1 cup warm water
- 1 package instant dry-yeast • 1 large egg • 1 Tablespoon honey
- ½ Tablespoon salt • 2 Tablespoons nuts, chopped • 1 cup grated mature cheese

    1 - Place wheat flour in a mixer bowl. Add yeast, and warm water. Mix for about 1/2 minute with dough hook.

    2 - Add salt, egg, honey and continue mixing. Add bread flour and continue mixing at a medium speed for at least 5 minutes to increase the gluten development.

    3 - Add grated cheese, and mix for 2 minutes. The dough should be soft to touch and not stick to the sides of the bowl.

    4 - Place dough in a large greased bowl, rolling the dough around to coat it on all sides. Cover with plastic wrap and let rise at a warm room temperature until doubled in size (about 3 hours).

    5 - To shape the dough into a loaf, breadsticks or rolls, use a little flour to coat your hands. Repeat step 4, and let rise again for ± 1 hour.

    6 - Preheat the oven to 350°F. Bake loaf for 30 minutes or until done (when tapping on the loaf, it should sound hollow). Bake breadsticks and rolls for ± 15-20 minutes.

    7 - Place on wire cooling racks, and let cool before cutting.

When using a bread machine, just follow the instructions of the machine to prepare the dough. TIP: Dough can be prepared in advance, refrigerated overnight or for up to three days, or placed in a freezer bag for up to 2 months.

Ingredients Mediterranean Cheese dough:

- 1 cup whole wheat flour • 2 cups bread flour • 1 cup warm water
- 1 package instant dry-yeast • 1 large egg • 1 Tablespoon honey
- ½ Tablespoon salt • Mediterranean seasoning: 1 teaspoon each of dried rosemary, basil, thyme, paprika • 1 cup grated Beemster® Nettle cheese

Follow same instructions to prepare the dough.

Veggie & Potato *Cheese* Gratin

Serves 4

Easy to prepare, 25 minutes in the oven, and dinner is ready. This is a dish created by my son Michael, who is a student, and is always looking for something easy to make that also fits into his budget. You can be creative and use any vegetables you have in your fridge.

You can also use different seasonings to change the flavor to your desire.

- 1 bunch carrots, washed
- 2 cups broccoli florets
- 2 cups cauliflower
- 4 medium red skin potatoes, cut into 1/2 inch thick slices
- 4 sprigs rosemary
- 1 Tablespoon Italian seasoning
- Salt & pepper to taste
- Gravy: 3 Tablespoon butter, melted, 1 Tablespoon gravy powder, $1/3$ cup water, mixed well
- 1 cup grated cheese of choice

1 - Preheat oven to 375°F/190°C.

2 - Place carrots, broccoli, cauliflower, potato slices and rosemary in an oven-safe dish. Sprinkle with Italian seasoning.

3 - Cover with aluminum foil.

4 - Place in pre-heated oven for ± 45-50 minutes until veggies and potato are almost 'al dente'.

5 - Pour gravy over the dish, cover with cheese and place dish back into the oven - uncovered for 5 minutes.

3 x Delicious *Cheese* Cookies

Makes 8-12

Crisp cookies with bold flavors are great as a small snack.

Ingredients Chipolte & Cheese Cookie:

- 1 puff pastry sheet (± 8x8 inch) • 1 teaspoon Chipolte pepper flakes
- ½ cup grated mature cheese, like a Beemster® Classic
- Eggwash: 1 egg beaten with 1 Tablespoon milk (use brush)
    1 - Pre-heat oven to 400°F/220°C.
    2 - Place pastry sheet on a cookie sheet or baking stone.
    3 - Cover with cheese, and sprinkle with pepper flakes.
    4 - Roll up, eggwash and cut into ¾ inch thick slices.
    5 - Place in pre-heated oven for ± 20-25 minutes until light golden brown.

Ingredients Pesto & Cheese Cookie:

- 1 puff pastry sheet (± 8x8 inch)
- ½ cup grated mature cheese • 1 Tablespoon pesto (see page 73)
- Eggwash: 1 egg beaten with 1 Tablespoon milk (use brush)
    1 - Pre-heat oven to 400°F/220°C.
    2 - Place pastry sheet on a cookie sheet or baking stone.
    3 - Spread pesto over the sheet, and cover with cheese.
    4 - Roll up, eggwash and cut into ¾ inch thick slices.
    5 - Place in pre-heated oven for ± 20-25 minutes until light golden brown.

Ingredients Sun-dried Tomato & Cheese Cookie:

- 1 puff pastry sheet (± 8x8 inch) • ¼ cup sun-dried tomato, chopped
- ½ cup grated young cheese, like a Beemster® Vlaskaas
- Eggwash: 1 egg beaten with 1 Tablespoon milk (use brush)
    1 - Pre-heat oven to 400°F/220°C.
    2 - Place pastry sheet on a cookie sheet or baking stone.
    3 - Cover with cheese and chopped sun-dried tomato.
    4 - Roll up, eggwash and cut into ¾ inch thick slices.
    5 - Place in pre-heated oven for ± 20-25 minutes until light golden brown.

Creamy *Prickly Pear Cactus* Sauce

Serves 4

This sauce is great with grilled beef or venison, and as a dessert sauce with frozen yogurt or ice cream of choice. The tangy flavor of the sauce is also great combined with a mature cheese, like Beemster® Classic or XO cheese.

Ingredients:

- 1 teaspoon butter
- 1 shallot, finely chopped
- 1 teaspoon garlic, minced
- 1 ½ cups prickly pear cactus pulp. Cut in half, scoop fruit
- ½ cup Orange based liqueur (Grand Marnier, Safari, Elizé)
- 2 Tablespoons light cream or H&H
- Salt & pepper to taste

  1 - Heat butter until melted, not browned. Add shallot and garlic. Stir until translucent.

  2 - Add fruit pulp, liqueur, cream and bring to taste with a little sea salt and pepper. On low heat, stir around for ± 2 minutes and well blended.

  3 - For a smooth sauce, force the puree through a medium to fine strainer.

Warm *Mixed Berries* Sauce

Serves 4

This sauce is great with grilled veal, chicken or pork, and as a dessert sauce with a warm pear, or ice cream; garnish with a mint leave. The sweetness of this sauce is also great combined with a young cheese, like Beemster® Vlaskaas, or a light mature cheese.

Ingredients:

- 2 cups mixed berries; strawberries, blackberries, blueberries, raspberries, currants
- ½ cup red wine

  1 - Heat skillet, add fruit and wine. Stir around on medium heat for ± 4 minutes.

  2 - Place in blender and blend until smooth.

Nutty *Cheese* Tuille

Makes ± 6-8

Ingredients:

- 1 cup coarsely grated mature cheese, like Beemster® Classic cheese
- 1 Tablespoon sesame seeds • 1 teaspoon wheat flour

1 - Pre-heat oven 325°F/165°C

2 - Mix cheese with sesame seeds and flour

3 - Place a mounded tablespoon of the mixture onto a non-stick cookie sheet or Silpat. Use a spoon to gently press the mound into a 2 inch circle. Allow at least 1 inch space between the tuilles.

4 - Place in pre-heated oven for 3-4 minutes, until light golden and bubbly.

5 - Let cool for 1 minute, remove with spatula, shape to desire, or keep flat for cookie shape. Store at room temperature.

To prepare a basket, let the tuille cool down for a few minutes before placing the tuille over a bowl and let it cool to harden.

Chunky *Fig* Chutney

Ingredients:

- 2 cups fresh figs, rinsed, stems removed, chopped coarsely • ½ cup port wine
- ½ cup brown sugar • ¼ cup fresh ginger, finely chopped
- 1 Tablespoon lemon zest • 1 teaspoon cinnamon • pinch sea salt
- ¼ teaspoon ground allspice

1 - Place all ingredients in saucepan. Bring to a boil, and let simmer for ± 30 minutes. Serve at room temperature.

Store in jar or container in refrigerator for up to 2 weeks.

Beemster® XO *Cheese* Pesto

Ingredients:

- 1 cup finely grated old cheese, like Beemster® XO cheese
- 2 Tablespoons garlic, minced • ¼ cup pinenuts
- 1 cup extra virgin olive oil • 4 cups basil leaves

1 - Place all ingredients in a blender until a smooth.

2 - Serve as a spread, or store in ice cube molds in freezer > 6 months.

73

Hoki with a Crunchy *Cheese* Crust

Serves 2

Hoki is a fish from New Zealand, comparable with cod or haddock. Check your freezer isle, at the store, for flash frozen Hoki. 'Flash frozen' means that the fish has been frozen at sea to preserve its flavor and smooth texture.

Ingredients:

- 2 Hoki filets
- 1 cup grated old cheese, like Beemster® XO
- 1 cup panko breadcrumbs
- 1 Tablespoon thyme
- Salt & pepper to taste
- Eggwash: 1 egg beaten with 1 teaspoon milk
- 1 Tablespoon all-purpose flour
- Oil to bake the fish

1 - MIx grated cheese, breadcrumbs, thyme an a little salt and pepper.
2 - Dredge the fish through the flour, coat both sides, shaking off excess.
3 - Put the floured fish into the egg wash.
4 - Lay the egg-coated filets onto a plate of cheese-breadcrumbs mix, and use your hand to pat the crumbs onto the fish.
5 - Heat oil in a skillet.
6 - Fry fish ± 4 minutes on both sides. Do not overcrowd the pan.

Serve with vegetables and starch of choice. A tartar or Ranch sauce goes very well with this flavor combination.

For an even bolder flavor, substitute Delft Blue cheese for the old grated cheese to prepare the crust. If choosing a blue cheese, omit the tartar sauce.

Beemster Classic is matured for no less than 18 months to ensure a wonderfully complex taste. The beautiful color of this cheese instantly reminds you of Carmel.

BEEMSTER Classic
Premium Gourmet Dutch Cheese

Classic was the first cheese from Beemster introduced to the United States and to this day remains the best selling Beemster cheese. Beemster Classic is the perfect age for any kind of cheese connoisseur to enjoy. One can enjoy Classic on a lunch sandwich in grade school or with fine wines at a dinner party.

Beemster XO is matured for 26 months making it Beemster's oldest cheese. Many people see 3-5 year old cheeses in stores and ask why we don't make an older product? Once you have tasted Beemster XO, the answer is quite simple.

BEEMSTER X·O·
Premium Gourmet Dutch Cheese

As a cheese matures, the flavors one tastes expands. As this process happens, moisture also exits, thus leaving the cheese tasting crumbly and granular in one's mouth. Because of Beemster's unique milk, XO is able to obtain one of the widest flavor ranges possible, in only 26 months, and still retains its smooth and creamy taste.

Beemster Vlaskaas is the newest addition to Beemster's line of Premium Gourmet Dutch Cheeses; however, it is the oldest cheese recipe within the group. When translated, Vlaskaas mean Flax cheese. This delightfully sweet and creamy cheese was made only during the harvest festival of the flax for the workers to eat on thick slices of bread and with porridge while they worked and celebrated.

Vlaskaas
The cheese with a rich tradition

While digging through the archives for the exact way to recreate the harvest cheese, the recipe for Vlaskaas was re-discovered. It was soon decided, that after generations of rest, it was time for Vlaskaas to live again! Renown for the best milk quality in The Netherlands, Beemster was asked to make the Vlaskaas recipe. The result was spectacular! Vlaskaas became the centerpiece of the entire harvest festival. Beemster Vlaskaas took home a Gold Medal in its category and 3rd place in the overall competition in the Wisconsin Cheese Makers Competition, which is regarded as the highest standard amongst cheese makers.

Beemster Lite Matured is the perfect alternative for cheese lovers who seek a true gourmet cheese. Beemster's philosophy has always been to bring the best possible taste to every consumer. Lite Matured achieves a superb taste with 33% less fat than an average "Gouda type" cheese. Finely, cheese lovers can have an afternoon cheese snack without feeling that they are ruining their diets.

BEEMSTERLITE Matured
Premium Gourmet Dutch Cheese

Beemster with Mustard Seed is a unique cheese with robust flavor. This cheese is sure to pleasantly surprise any audience. Beemster with Mustard Seed is a superb addition to hamburgers on the grill or any dish where the added texture of the mustard seeds can be appreciated.

Beemster with Garlic is a 'dream come true' for garlic lovers. This cheese is so smooth and creamy, yet provides a natural Garlic taste. Beemster with Garlic melts wonderfully and is a great addition to any sandwich or melted on top of a soup.

Beemster with Nettles provides a wonderfully refreshing taste that is always sure to please.

Many consumers in the USA have never heard of stinging nettles or else have been taught to stay away from this pain causing plant. However, for generations in Europe, nettle has been providing herbal medication once it is cut and left to dry.

Nettles are a common ingredient in soups and teas throughout Europe, and it known that Nettle has a wonderful effect on the body and helps increase blood circulation.

Cheese Making history

On July 7th, 2006, a large crowd watched intensely as the forklift got into position to remove the cheese from the horse-drawn wagon. The enormous wheel was carefully lowered onto the traditional custom's house scales.

The representative from the Guinness Book of World Records stood by as weights were added to bring the wheel of cheese off of the ground to an equilibrium on the historic scale.

At 1,323 lbs. the scale was balanced! When the weight of the cheese was announced by the Master Cheese-Maker, the crowd of spectators cheered and applauded.

The Master Cheese-Maker tasted and approved this three-month-old wheel. The Cheese Carriers' Guild gathered around the cheese to have a taste and help move the 600.5 Kg wheel to the middle of the square.

More then 6,000 liters of milk were used and, a special hand made wood mold was created in order to craft this wheel of cheese. For more information visit www.beemstercheese.us

What you should know about cheese

Q: How should I keep cheese refrigerated?

A: Cheese should be refrigerated at temperatures between 40°F –
45°F in the original wrapping or container, in a plastic zip bag, or a
tightly covered container.

Q: At what temperature should my cheese be served?

A: The flavor of Beemster® is best when eaten at room temperature.
Remove from refrigerator at least 1 to 2 hours, in advance of serving.

Q: If cheese gets moldy, should I throw it away?

A: Mold may develop on the surface of cheese. Although most molds
are harmless, to be safe, cut away 1/2 inch of cheese on all sides that
have visible mold. Use the remaining cheese as quickly as possible.

**Q: What are the white dots that appear in the more aged
Beemster® cheeses?**

A: These are protein crystals that develop when the cheese
matures. Cheese connoisseurs appreciate these dots very much.
They are a sign that the cheese has ripened extremely well.

Q: Can I eat the rind of Beemster®?

A: No. The rind protects the cheese from dehydrating and molding.
The rind partially consists of a plastic coating that does not digest.

Q: What makes the holes in the cheese?

A: During the cheese-making process, cultures are added to the milk
that produces a gas. The gas that forms the holes is carbon
dioxide, and Beemster® use cultures that make relatively more
holes than average Gouda cheeses.

Q: Is Beemster made using vegetable rennet or animal rennet?

A: Beemster is made using animal rennet.

Recipes per cheese type

Young cheese, like Beemster Vlaskaas, Edam, young Gouda

Potato Gratin d'Provence	12
Beans & Cheese Salad	15
Fruit & Cheese Kebabs	19
Mandarin & Cheese Salad	21
Cheese Tuna Melt Canape	47
Surprising Cheese Pouches	49
Beemster® Vlaskaas Cheese Fondue	51
Colorful Macaroni & Cheese	52
Belgium Beer & Cheese Stew	56
Spinach & Cheese Soup	58
Red Lentils & Cheese Soup	58
3 x Delicious Cheese Cookie	68

Farmers Cheese

Spinach & Cheese Meatloaf	27

Herbal Cheese, like Beemster Mustard Cheese

Spicy Sausage & Cheese Flatbread	39
Three Cheese Ravioli	62

Herbal Cheese, like Beemster Nettle Cheese

Extravagant Seafood Pasta	31
Grilled Cheese Panini	61
Whole Wheat & Cheese Bread Delights	65

Herbal Cheese, like Beemster Garlic Cheese

Corn & Cheese Delights	10
Fruit & Cheese Kebabs	19
Shrimp & Cheese Stuffed Hot Peppers	35
Garlic Cheese with Roast Beef Canape	47

Blue Cheese, like Delft Blue

Delft Blue Chicken Oven Dish	33
Scrumptious Cobb Salad	40
Zucchini, Beef & Cheese Carpaccio	42
Three Cheese Ravioli	62
Hoki with a Crunchy Cheese Crust	75

Mature, Extra Mature, like Beemster Classic

Prosciutto & Cheese Puff Pastry Fun	9
Scandinavian Smoked Salmon Roses	16
Fruit & Cheese Kebabs	19
Deep Dish Cheese & Veggie Pie	28
Onion, Garlic & Cheese Scones	35
Gorgeous Cheese Tower	37
Surprising Cheese Pouches	49
Impressionable Oyster Gratin	54
Grilled Cheese Panini	61
Whole Wheat & Cheese Bread Delights	65
3 x Delicious Cheese Cookie	68
Nutty Cheese Tuille	73

Old Crumble Cheese, like Beemster XO

Belgium Endive & Cheese Gratin	12
Gorgeous Cheese Tower	37
Zucchini, Beef & Cheese Carpaccio	42
Three Cheese Ravioli	62
Beemster® XO Cheese Pesto	73
Hoki with a Crunchy Cheese Crust	75

Cream Cheese

Cream Cheese Wontons	16
Gorgeous Cheese Tower	37

Goat Cheese, like Chèvre

Colorful Chèvre Potato Salad	25
Refreshing Chèvre & Pear Salad	25

Cheese of Choice

Party Cheese Shapes	16
Ham & Cheese Profiterole	19
Salmon & Cheese Lasagna	22
Gorgeous Cheese Tower	37
Tuna, Eggplant & Cheese 'Frittata'	45
Smoked Salmon Canape	47
Veggie & Potato Gratin	67

More books in the 'Get Real Healthy Food' Series are:

"*Amazing* **7** *Minute Meals*"

"Knowing what's in your food,
is the key to healthy
weight loss and
weight management.
Make it yourself:
No trans-fatty fats, no enriched
flours,
no hidden chemicals;
just delicious flavors!

"That is what I will teach
you in "Amazing **7** *Minute Meals"*
- Yvonne Stephens

And the <u>faster</u> you cook it, the <u>slower it is being digested</u>!

Healthy, easy to prepare recipes from all over the world, ready in 7 minutes or less. Learn how to cut up veggies, bell peppers etc., when you have time, so when you're busy, you only have to spend 7 minutes to prepare a delicious, healthy meal.

Order your own "Amazing 7 Minute Meals" book online at www.getrealhealthyfood.com

Our online price per book including S&H (Priority Mail) is $ 22.95.

You can have your book(s) personalized by Chef Yvonne Stephens.

Please sign up for our newsletter, with recipes and information about new books in our series, like the soon to be released, "Just Try Fish."